Painters of Pukatawagan
Mathias Colomb Cree Nation

I0478526

Sharona Caribou

Copyright © 2012 Sharona Caribou

All rights reserved.

ISBN:1540628035
ISBN-13:9781540628039

DEDICATION

I WOULD LIKE TO DEDICATE THIS BOOK FOR THE YOUNG GENERATION AND MANY OTHER FUTURE GENERATIONS OF PUKATAWAGAN, MANITOBA.

EVERYONE HAS THE CHANCE TO BECOME A PAINTNER, NOBODY CAN'T TELL YOU THAT YOU CANNOT PAINT. IT DOES TAKES TIME AND PATIENCE, VERY MUCH THOUGHT TO BRING CREATIVITY AND COLOR TOGETHER.

PAINTING IS NOT ABOUT MAKING MONEY, IT BRINGS JOY, HAPPINESS AND EVEN MORE THE COMPLIMENTS YOU WOULD RECEIVE FROM OTHERS.

NO MATTER HOW OLD OR YOUNG YOU MAY BE, YOUR BORN WITH TALENT, BUT JUST NOT YET DISCOVERED, BUT SOMEDAY OR HOUR YOU WILL SOON FIND YOUR TALENT WHETHER IT'S PAINTING OR NOT.

MY BOOK IS ABOUT THESE PAINTERS FOR THE BEAUTIFUL ARTWORK THEY CREATED AND THE JOY IT BRINGS OTHERS.

CONTENTS

ACKNOWLEDGMENTS

I would like to thanks to my sponsor agency Pukatawagan Education Authority
Clare Hart
For giving me the opportunity to attend UCN located here in Pukatawagan,
Manitoba.
Also Thanks to my instructor Janice Seto for the help of making this booklet
and Ralph Caribou for his acknowledgment.
I would like to also Thank Edward Colomb, Dino Colomb, , Shannon Colomb
and Roman Bighetty for their time in helping me complete my booklet about
Art Talent In pukatawagan.

Edward Colomb resident of Pukatawagan, Northern, Manitoba, Mathias Colomb Cree Nation.

Edward started off by drawing at the age of 9 years old, Using pencil crayons, Self Taught how to mix colors and to be familiar with the outcome. His inspiration came from a tv program who aired Bob Ross. As he got older, he began to start using paint in the 1980's. He was fascinated with mother nature's scenery like forestry, wolves, bears, and the midnight skies. To him painting is not a job, he considers it as a hobby. When he's painting he goes into his own world of feeling happy and comfortable of his artwork. Over the years his talent grew, his work was recognized by others. Edward got asked to paint the Nikawiy Health Centre and many other buildings. Edward says "painting just comes naturally and it's in the blood" he is proud of his artwork that he has done over the years. Someday he said he wants to give oil painting a try.

Art Work BY: **Edward Colomb**

Art Work BY: Edward Colomb

Roman Bighetty, Resident of Pukatawagan Northern Manitoba, Mathias Colomb Cree Nation. Roman started painting at the age of 25, by painting on his homemade earrings, he was interested in painting on canvas. Gino Colomb took the time to show Roman how to stroke and keep the paint brushes clean. Also learned how to mix colors by watching Dino and Gino Colomb paint. He then taught himself how to mix colors and paint the right way. Roman doesn't see painting as a hobby, he waits till someone requests a painting by him. He his excited to see his creation when he is done, looks forward in seeing the artwork. On his spare time he's a crafty guy, he also enjoys making regalias and doing bead work and sewing. he always busy with his time. for the near future he decides to still be painting.

Painting by : **Roman Bighetty**

he painted these by request using plywood and paint.

Heres another 3 plywood painting , he got asked to cut and paint.
Artwork BY: Roman Bighetty

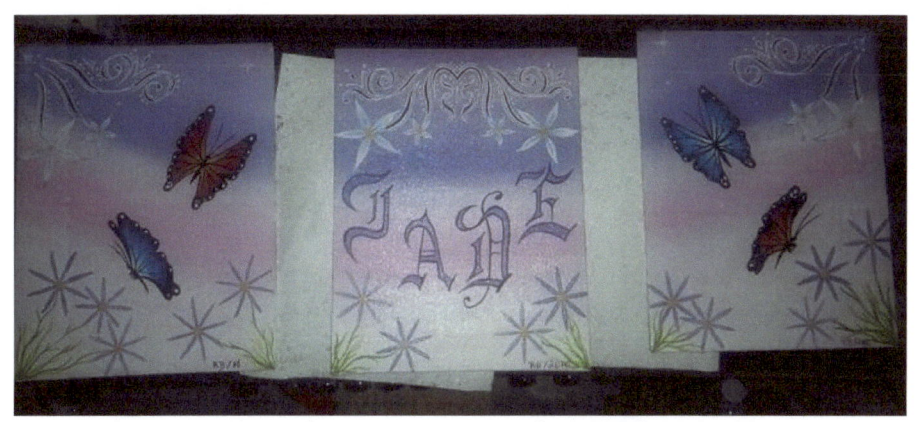

Here's another painting he did on canvas.
Artwork by :Roman Bighetty

Plywood Painting BY : Roman Bighetty

Dino Colomb a resident of Pukatwagan, Northern Manitoba of Mathias Colomb Cree Nation. Edward started off by drawing with paper and pencil crayons at the age of 15, was interested in trying painting.

He was inspired by Brad Castel who showed him how to mix colors and Solomon Colomb who taught him how to do detail work.

Dino is now 31 years old and enjoys painting as a hobby. He gets a good feeling about his Artwork, the compliments and requests he gets, Mostly feeling good about being self-employed. Getting contracts to paint on his spare time.

Dino and his dad Edward colomb and twin brother Gino Colomb have art work done in most Northern Communities right to British Colombia down, to Ireland. He continues to still paint and someday get a business going for painting contracts and be called "Tree Lines"

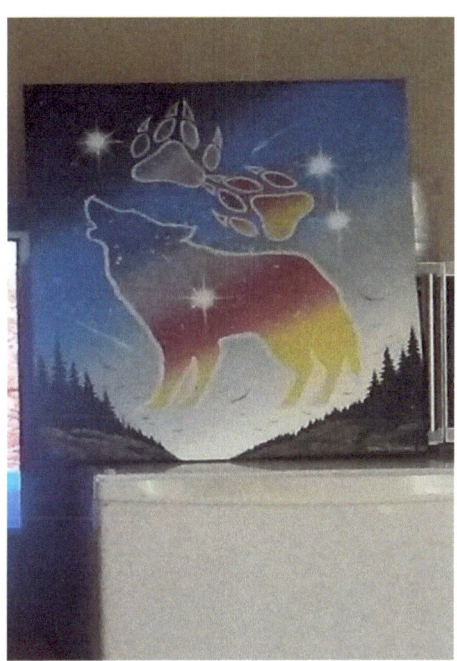

Here's another picture of Dino's artwork. Hanging in a ladies home.

Dino Colomb and his artwork. He also did other work in work field places, pictures will be shown below.

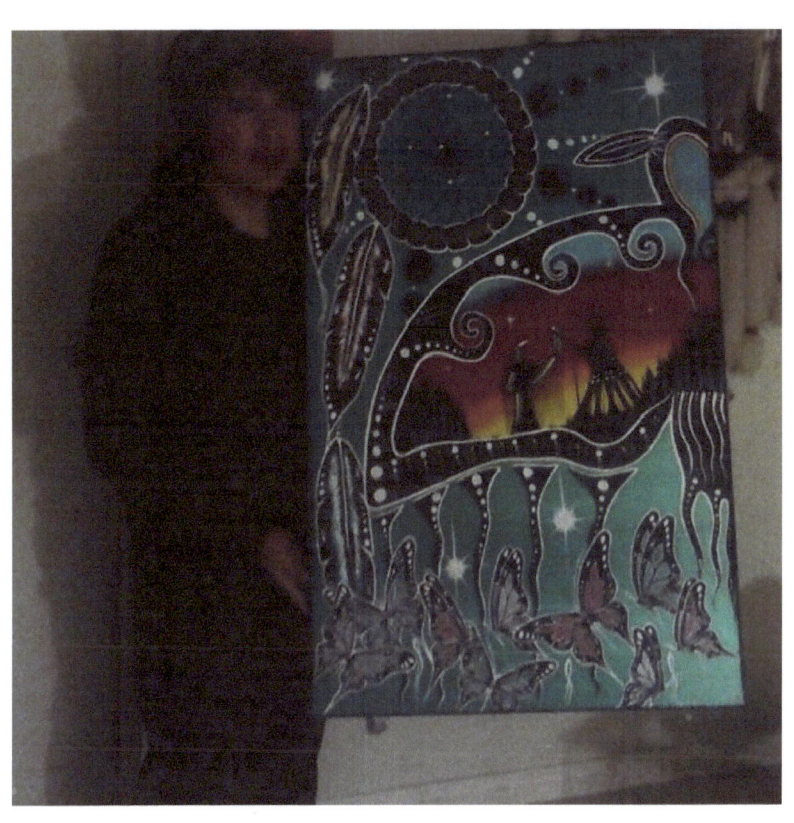

Photo of Shannon Colomb and her Artwork

HERE ARE SOME PAINTING WITH BRIGHT COLORS AND DETAIL WORK.

ART WORK BY: SHANNON COLOMB

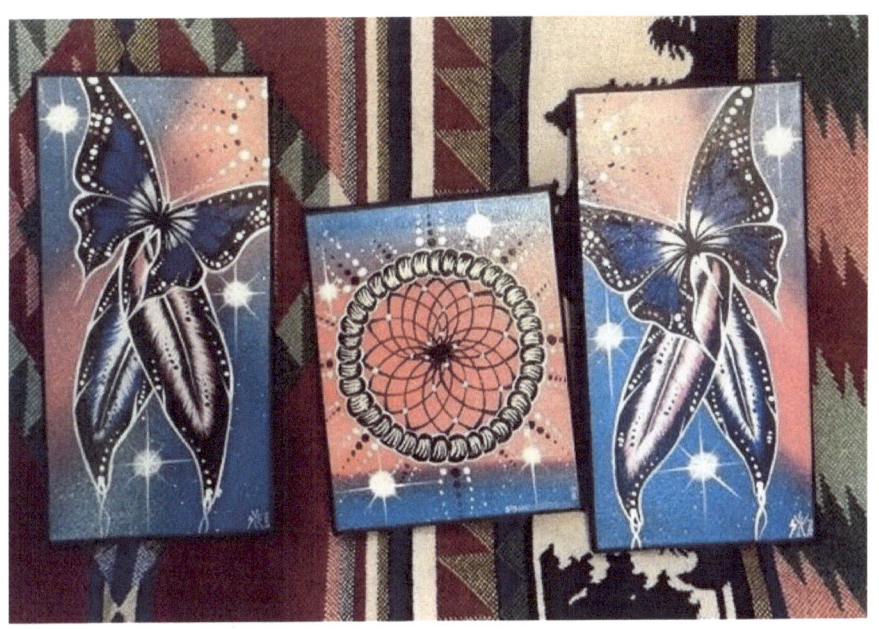

I love these 3 canvas painting, how the color flows, and the beautiful outcome of it.
ArtWork By: Shannon Colomb

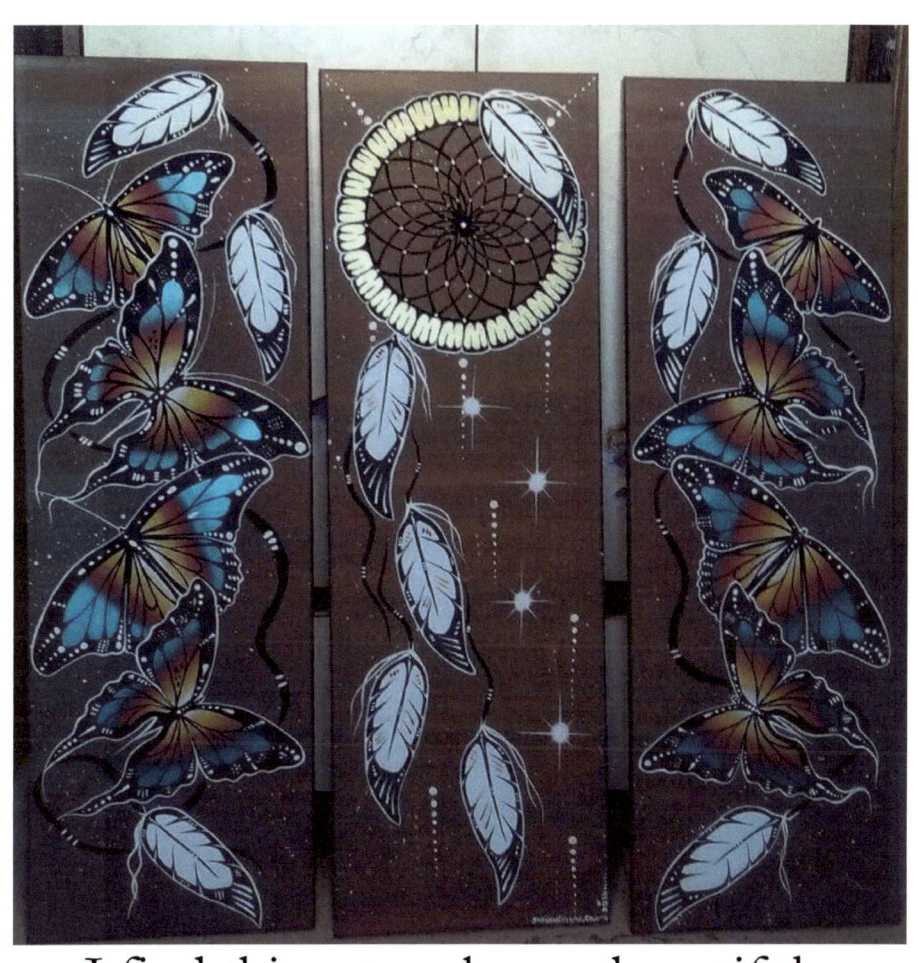

I find this artwork very beautiful.
BY: Shannon Colomb

These Pictures of the building inside of the artwork done by Edward Colomb, Dino and Gino Colomb, Roman Bighetty are from The M.C.C.N Band Office.

These are border lines that go all around the band office.
These Photos are from The Nikawiy Health
Center, also border lines that go

all around the entire building.

Painting by Shannon Colomb

Art Work by: Shannon Colomb

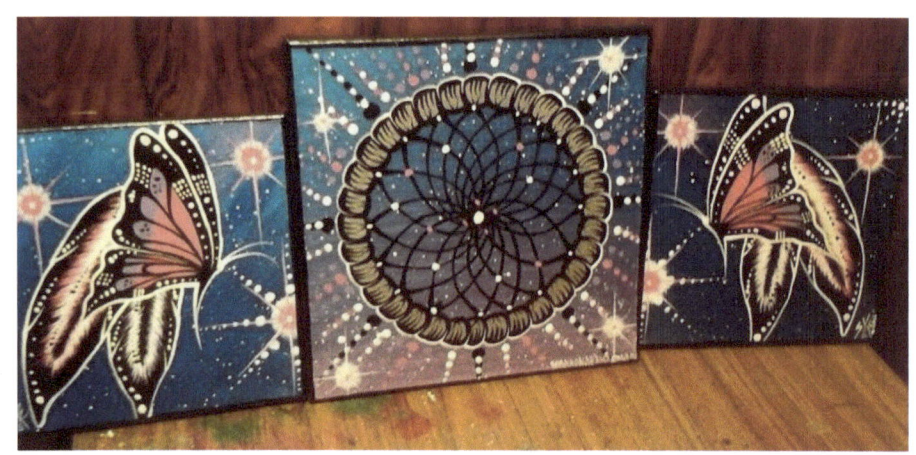

Artwork done by:Shannon Colomb

Artwork by :Shannon Colomb

Artwork by : Shannon Colomb

ABOUT THE AUTHOR

Sharona Caribou, Graduated from Kelsey Learning Centre, The Pas, MB, Now attending as a student at University College of The North in Pukatawagan, MB of Mathias Colomb Cree Nation.

I'm 25 years old, A mother of 3 beautiful children. My interests are sports and exploring new things outside my comfort zone. I intend to push myself over the limits, But mostly have fun while I'm learning. Everyone in the community as well as out of the community people are fascinated by painting, The colors and designs how they could merge together brings a beautiful outcome or image what they desire. The art work would be recognized by others. My book is dedicated for the people with amazing painting talent who resides In Pukatawagan, MB home of Mathias Colomb Cree Nation.

Ekosi